Original title:
The Ivy's Secret

Copyright © 2025 Creative Arts Management OÜ
All rights reserved.

Author: Evan Hawthorne
ISBN HARDBACK: 978-1-80581-889-2
ISBN PAPERBACK: 978-1-80581-416-0
ISBN EBOOK: 978-1-80581-889-2

Entwined Histories of Nature

In the garden, a tale is spun,
Leaves gossip about the sun.
Rabbits dance with a sprightly flair,
While squirrels borrow without a care.

Vines twist like a playful frown,
Claiming space in a merry gown.
Flowers chuckle, their colors bright,
In this leafy world, pure delight.

The Lattice of Life's Secrets

Beneath the lattice, stories hide,
A sneaky snail on a slippery ride.
Ladybugs laugh at their own burr,
While ants discuss the next big fur.

A jolly breeze sways the stalks,
Tickling the leaves, oh how it mocks!
Bees are buzzing their silly tune,
As petals sway and faintly swoon.

Trellis of Time's Memories

A trellis stands, tall and proud,
Its stories are whispered, never loud.
With each twist and each leafy curl,
It holds the memories of the world.

There's a bug who tells a grand old tale,
Of a daring jump—and a near-failed sail.
But grasshoppers laugh at the clumsy flops,
As they leap about, right over the tops.

Secrets Beneath the Canopy

Under the canopy, laughter runs,
Where secrets sprout and joy weighs tons.
A wise old owl hoots a witty pun,
While tiny mice plot their nightly fun.

Frogs croak symphonies in the night,
As fireflies twinkle, a sparkling sight.
Every leaf holds a hilarious quip,
In this wild world, on a laughter trip.

Monuments of the Forgotten Grove

In a grove where trees pretend,
Lies a monument, my dear friend.
With squirrels stealing all the hype,
It's a statue of a very shy type.

Whispers echo through the leaves,
As the breeze plays tricks, it retrieves.
A face carved in bark, oh what a sight!
Looks like he lost a feather in flight.

Rabbits dance around in glee,
Who knew fur could be so free?
They laugh and tumble, a furry squad,
Yet the old statue just gives a nod.

A picnic's happening, crumbs in the air,
A raccoon steals a sandwich with flair.
While the monument stays all still,
"Here's living proof, I need a chill!"

The Silent Echoes of Climbing Fronds

Vines are tangled, quite a sight,
A green hotel for bugs at night.
They chatter and clatter with such delight,
While the fronds chuckle, what a fright!

A snail pops by, wearing a crown,
He thinks the vines won't let him down.
"Fast or slow, I'll take my time,
This leafy race is truly sublime!"

Lizards glide with a wink and a twist,
Slinking around as if they've missed.
The fronds do cheer, "Join us for fun,
In this leafy game, we all are one!"

Then comes the rain, what a splash!
The bugs dive in, oh what a crash!
As puddles form, they swim with glee,
In this jungle, wild and free!

The Green Whispering Wall

In the garden, green and bright,
Whispers travel day and night.
Leaves giggle, branches sway,
Sharing secrets in a playful way.

Shadows dance and roots entwine,
A green wall that reads like a sign.
What's behind this leafy maze?
A plant's prank, in winding ways.

Laughter flows from every creak,
Softly spoken, yet quite cheek.
A gnome hides with a cheeky grin,
Planning mischief with a spin.

Oh, the stories plants could tell,
Of picnic bugs and ringing bells.
With every rustle, charm ignites,
Underneath the starry nights.

Secrets in the Twisting Vines

Twisting vines with tales quite tall,
A mismatched shoe, a garden ball.
Secrets hidden in every curl,
Watch them giggle, twirl, and whirl.

A bumblebee's gossip, oh what fun,
About the squash who thinks he's won.
With wigs made of leafy lace,
They prance around, a merry race.

Frogs in tuxedos, such a sight,
Leap through the air, taking flight.
In this vine-clad jubilee,
All the plants sing joyfully.

Rustling leaves, they join the song,
A wacky world where all belong.
Under the moon, a vine parade,
With chuckles through the plans they've made.

Beneath Emerald Canopies

Beneath the leaves, a world of cheer,
As squirrels dance and drink their beer.
Caterpillars wearing hats,
Join in line with chatty bats.

A picnic spread with crumbs galore,
Squeaky mice that dance on floor.
Every shade a slice of fun,
'Til all is lost—oh, what a run!

Under emerald canopies high,
A world where whispers tickle the sky.
Rabbits wearing shoes quite rare,
Hop in rhythm without a care.

Crisp cool breeze with teasing laughs,
Hiding mice and snapping staffs.
In this place where green delights,
Fun unfolds in leafy sights.

Tales Twisted by Twirls

Tales twisted with a vine-y twist,
From spinning tops to the autumn mist.
A hedgehog wears a fancy coat,
As laughter rides on every note.

Around the curves and charming bends,
Every plant has merry friends.
A secret club, they chit and chat,
While plotting pranks, imagine that!

Twirl and swirl, the dandelions play,
Sharing giggles as they sway.
A cabbage rolls, the crowd does cheer,
In this garden, fun's sincere.

Round and round the tales unfold,
In whispers soft and laughter bold.
In every leaf, a playful hint,
Of wild adventures the plants imprint.

Lush Cloaks of Deception

In the garden, whispers flow,
Leaves dressed up in charming show.
They wear capes of vibrant green,
But what lies under? Unseen, unseen!

Beneath the smiles, a riddle plays,
Were they there for sunny days?
Or were they plotting sneaky schemes,
As they shade our wildest dreams?

Who knew green could play such tricks?
With tangled vines as wicked picks?
What fun it is to tease and twist,
The plants conspire and laugh with a hiss!

So stroll along with a wink and grin,
In nature's game, we all can win.
For laughter lurks in leafy talks,
Where secrets bloom and no one walks!

Glistening Clusters of Truth

Beneath the boughs of verdant shade,
Little gems in sunlight played.
Each droplet clings with a cheeky cheer,
But are they truth or just a smear?

Nature giggles behind her veil,
With sparkles like a sailor's tale.
"Is it rain or fairy dust?" they tease,
While we wipe our eyes on the breeze!

Clusters glimmer in the soft light's call,
Hiding secrets, both big and small.
Are they friends or foes in disguise?
On this journey, will we capsize?

So let's all dive, don't be afraid,
Join the dance the foliage made.
For truth is sweet among the jest,
In the garden's heart, let's be a guest!

Tendrils of Intrigue

Twisted vines with mischief in mind,
Plotting chaos, oh so unkind.
With curls and loops, they pull and tug,
As if the plants all share a hug!

They stretch and sway, weaving their plot,
Bringing joy—maybe, maybe not!
"Are you with me?" they slyly ask,
Or will you in their riddles bask?

Around the garden, laughter soars,
As we peek through leafy doors.
With every tendril, a new delight,
Shining softly in moonlit night!

So dance with vines, take the bait,
Embrace the twists, don't hesitate!
In this riddle of green delight,
Let's solve together through the night!

Echoes in the Foliage

Listen closely, what's that sound?
Echoes hide where leaves abound.
With rustles, chuckles, they conspire,
Frolic merrily, never tire!

Hushed secrets shared among the trees,
Carried softly on the breeze.
"Did you hear?" they whisper low,
While giggling leaves put on a show!

Nature's jesters, oh so sly,
With every rustle, secrets fly.
Like cheeky sprites who love a game,
Each sound unique, none quite the same!

So wander forth, my playful friend,
Let echoes guide you, don't pretend.
In the foliage, laughs await,
Where mischief dances, let's celebrate!

Lush Labyrinths of Solitude

In the maze where hedges grow,
I lost my way, but please don't blow.
The whispers tell, the vines all tease,
Oh, to find my way with ease!

With every turn, a rabbit grins,
A squirrel nods, the mischief wins.
The path stretches on, my legs do tire,
Yet laughter blooms, lifting my ire.

I swear I saw a dancing cat,
With shades of green, it wore a hat.
"Join the fun!" it called with glee,
But all I want is to eat my tea!

So here I wander, lost in jest,
Each leaf a joker, nature's quest.
I'll take my time, make no regret,
In this tangle, I'm surely set!

Echoes Beneath the Boughs

Beneath the branches, chatter flows,
A chorus of chuckles where nobody knows.
A bird takes flight, a breezy quack,
As I chase shadows, I can't get back!

"Hey there, friend, do you need a map?"
A raccoon winks; I feel the trap.
I'm tangled up in leafy cheer,
A rabbit sneezes—oh dear, oh dear!

An owl hoots low with a wise old grin,
"Take a left, my friend, then spin!"
But every turn brings me more gags,
I trip and tumble, fate in rags.

So I'll embrace this silly fate,
With every laugh, I celebrate.
In echoes deep, where fun's the key,
Who knew lost could feel so free?

Unspoken Dialogues Among the Leaves

The leaves convene with a rustling sigh,
"Might we prank the guy passing by?"
With every flitter, a giggling tune,
In secret talks beneath the moon.

A branch drops low, a game of tease,
"Hey, don't step there; it's full of bees!"
A chuckle bursts in the quiet night,
The trees have humor, their delight!

Pine needles shrug with a wink and smile,
"Join the jest, stay for a while!"
With each new trick, I'm caught off guard,
But the laughter flows; it's not that hard.

So here I stand, in nature's cheer,
Amidst the whispers, I have no fear.
With every leaf that tickles and plays,
I find myself lost in joyful ways.

Entangled in Nature's Whisper

In the garden where shadows creep,
Vines tangle and secrets keep.
A gnome peeks out with a friendly grin,
"Don't step too hard; let's not begin!"

The flowers gossip, petals aflutter,
"Who misplaced all this garden clutter?"
With butterflies critiquing the design,
I can't help but laugh, it's all so fine!

The wind joins in with a cheeky blow,
Sending leaves dancing; what a show!
I chase the swirls, my feet a mess,
In this whimsical jumble, I must confess.

So I'll dive in where whimsy grows,
And let the joy of nature flows.
Tangled and lost but having a ball,
To be part of this laughter—who could want more after all?

The Whims of the Wandering Vines

In a garden where laughter twines,
The vines tell tales in crooked lines.
They tickle the trees, they tease the ground,
Whispering secrets with giggles all around.

They dance on fences, they swing so free,
Climbing up walls just to take a peek.
A leaf here, a curl there, a playful climb,
Crafting their own silly nursery rhyme.

They frolic and tumble in brilliant green,
Nature's jesters in a leafy scene.
With roots that wiggle and tendrils that play,
Creating mischief in a grand ballet.

So if you wander where the shadows fall,
Catch a glimpse of the vines having a ball.
In their funny antics, you'll surely find,
Laughter echoes, with nature intertwined.

Stories Woven in Green

Once upon a creeping vine,
Spun a tale of a silly swine.
He tried to dance, but slipped in mud,
And his friends laughed loud, what a thud!

A squirrel joined in, with acorn hat,
Danced a jig on a branch so fat.
The leaves were clapping, the winds did cheer,
As nature's comedy band gathered near.

Each twist and twirl, a chapter unfolds,
In the whispers of green, where laughter holds.
The flowers chuckled, the sun, it smiled,
In this playful saga, nature's own child.

So listen closely, when you're out on a stroll,
For the vines have stories, and they take a toll.
With giggles and gasps, they'll spin you around,
In the world of the green, pure fun can be found.

Intricacies of Nature's Fabric

Woven softly in shades of glee,
Nature's fabric giggles knowingly.
The threads of green play hide and seek,
In every nook, a poke, a peek.

A bumblebee buzzes, in stitches so fine,
Stitching laughter into the vine.
The daisies join in with their bright little heads,
Sprinkling humor where the sunlight treads.

Oh, the curls and the loops, oh, what a sight,
Each tangling twist a joyful delight.
From roots to leaves, they conspire, you see,
Together they weave a tapestry of glee.

In this fabric of fun, nature entwines,
Creating a riddle in playful designs.
So take a moment, and you might uncover,
The quirks of the green, like a captivating lover.

The Labyrinth of the Living Green

In a labyrinth where the green vines play,
A twisty path leads the lost astray.
With each turn taken, a giggle is found,
Nature's jokes echoing all around.

A hedgehog hitches a comical ride,
Through tangled trails, with pride, he slides.
He teeters and wobbles, giving a shout,
'Who knew weeds could lead to this kind of rout?'

The sun peeks through, in stripes of delight,
As laughter blooms with the morning light.
Every leaf whispers a pun or two,
In this living maze, both fresh and new.

So if you dare to wander these lanes,
Bring your sense of humor; bring your refrains.
In the riddle of nature, let joy be the key,
In the labyrinth of green, there's fun, you see!

Nature's Veiled Mystery

In shadows green, a riddle grows,
With leaves that hide all sorts of woes.
A squirrel chuckles, tail in the air,
While bugs debate who gets to share.

The sun peeks in, a cheeky grin,
While petals giggle, "Let's begin!"
They toss a dance, a waltz divine,
But wait, what's that? A slithery line!

Secrets Wrapped in Twine

A twisty vine, like gossip spread,
Whispers secrets of things long dead.
A snail slips by, in royal glee,
Carrying tales of a bumblebee.

"Did you hear?" the daisies say,
"Last week the wind just flew away!"
Rustling leaves join in the fun,
As nature giggles under the sun.

The Heart of the Climber

With grit and grace, the climber swings,
Clutching life by its awkward strings.
Each upward gasp, a twist of fate,
As ants declare it's getting late.

"Oh dear," they shout, "where's the cheese?"
The climber jokes, "Just find the trees!"
And up he goes, a clown on high,
While birds all laugh as they fly by.

Forgotten Tales of the Arbor

In the old oak, a tale is spun,
Of acorns lost and squirrels on the run.
"Remember when," a crow caws loud,
"Your nuts fell straight, but mine were proud?"

With branches swaying, laughter blooms,
As shadows dance in leafy rooms.
The woodpecker drums a silly beat,
While raccoons plot their next sweet treat.

Covert Lives in the Canopy

In the trees where squirrels peek,
Gossip flies, oh what a sneak!
The leaves are rustling with delight,
Secrets shared by day and night.

A crow drops in, with tales to tell,
Of hidden nuts and who fell fell!
Bamboo whispers, laughter's sound,
In this leafy lair, joy abounds.

Raccoons dance, they have a ball,
While owls pretend they know it all.
High up, the branches hold their glee,
This canopy's a comedy!

With roots that tangle and vines that twist,
No garden party could be missed.
A party hidden from the eye,
In leafy realms, the critters lie.

The Ivy's Silent Counsel

Whispers in the greenish glow,
Comfy spots where breezes blow.
Rabbits giggle, snickering slight,
As ivy shares its wise insight.

Forget the fuss of daily strife,
In leafy shade, we share our life.
With every climb comes a sly grin,
The more you peek, the more you win.

Twirling vines, they can't keep still,
Each twist a chance, a rogue thrill.
Around the trunk, a game we play,
As critters gather and sway away.

Frogs leap forth to crack a joke,
With every croak, the laughter stoked.
In this realm of ivy's grace,
We poke fun in leafy space!

Lattice of Secrets

A lattice woven green and grand,
Where secrets tossed like grain of sand.
Bees buzz in on silly quests,
Searching for the best, the best!

The whispers tickle as they weave,
More mischief than you can believe.
Caterpillars boast of a new sale,
On tasty greens, they'll never pale!

In tangled knots, the jesters prance,
A comedy of chance and dance.
Vines embrace, a slippery trip,
Nature's laughter, not a blip.

Oh, what stories wrapped in green,
The funniest scenes there ever been!
Through the lattice, giggings glide,
In this wild world, joy can't hide.

Cryptic Growths

Mossy patches hide their cheer,
With every creak and whispered sneer.
Snails ponder on their slimy trails,
Crafting jokes in leafy gales.

Beneath the ferns, a party brews,
Where every critter finds their muse.
Jokes on bugs too slow to dash,
In the quick of night, they all clash.

Treetop tales that twirl and spin,
With branches swing, what a grin!
Spider webs catch giggles bright,
In their silken threads, pure delight.

Cryptic growths, they laugh and tease,
In tangled green, they find their ease.
With nature's wit as their delight,
The world unfolds in pure moonlight.

Lurking in the Green Abyss

In the garden, things conspire,
Vines are creeping, never tire.
Lurking laughter fills the air,
Green mischief everywhere.

Gnomes peek from behind the leaves,
Plotting tricks that none believes.
Snakes in hats take tea at dawn,
Winking as they play along.

Frogs in tuxedos dance with flair,
While mice recite a sonnet rare.
Under twinkling, starry skies,
The shyest blooms wear silly ties.

So if you stroll through leafy lanes,
Beware of plants that jest and feigns.
For laughter springs from verdant beds,
And secrets churn in leafy spreads.

The Enchantment of Twisting Paths

Winding trails with whispered glee,
Lead to secrets, can you see?
Twisted vines with coats of charm,
Embrace the trees, but cause alarm.

Spiders spin a web of jokes,
While squirrels plot like sneaky folks.
A scarecrow grins beneath the sun,
With cornstalk eyes, it's all in fun.

Flowers giggle, petals wide,
As bees buzz by, a joyful ride.
Nature plays its merry tune,
While frogs croak like it's high noon.

So wander through, just take a chance,
Join in on this leafy dance.
Where every twist is bright and bold,
And laughter's worth its weight in gold.

In the Grasp of the Vines

Wrapped in greens, a secret throng,
Vines are weaving all day long.
Tickling toes and brushing knees,
Whispers riding on the breeze.

Laughter echoes, roots entwined,
Hidden jokes are hard to find.
A caterpillar winks with glee,
As bugs all dance on tipsy spree.

Vines make hats, a leafy style,
As hedgehogs giggle all the while.
Fanciful gowns on flowers sway,
As nature hosts a grand ballet.

So if you find yourself enmeshed,
In the larks that all are fresh,
Remember here, where laughter's loud,
The vines keep secrets, oh so proud.

Shadows of the Forgotten Garden

In shadows deep, a garden sleeps,
Where giggling flowers hide in heaps.
Faded paths in colors bright,
Whisper tales of silly fright.

A polka-dot toad in a hat,
Wonders where the ginger cat.
With every tick of time, it seems,
Night blooms sprout with funny dreams.

Beasts that steal the gardener's shovel,
Make mischief in a leafy hovel.
Echoes dance where moonlight gleams,
In a world of playful schemes.

So when the shadows softly lean,
Join the fun where life's unseen.
For laughter's wild in twilight's hold,
A blissful garden, bright and bold.

The Tapestry of Life Unseen

In gardens where the secrets bloom,
Tangled whispers lift the gloom,
A gnome with a hat, quite absurdly fat,
Watches the world with a goofy zoom.

Each leaf a tale of evening bets,
With squirrels dressed in tiny vests,
They judge the bees for their clumsy spree,
As pollen dust their fuzzy pets.

The flowers gossip, laughter rings,
About the antics of tiny things,
A frog in a bog sings out a fog,
While the moonlight winks and swings.

Oh, the mysteries that nature holds,
In stories brief, yet rarely told,
Where vines align in silly design,
And laughter is the best of gold.

Vines of Unfathomable Truth

Through tangled vines of grape and vine,
Lies a riddle, a goofy sign,
A slug in a hat, next to a mat,
Claims to know the punchline fine.

With whispers soft, the leaves collide,
As critters gather for the ride,
A raccoon in boots, tapping his roots,
Says, 'Join the party, don't you hide!'

Laughter echoes in every nook,
As rabbits read from a silly book,
They dance in pairs, with mismatched flares,
While squirrels plot their sneaky hook.

It's not just earth; it's a comedy show,
Where every chat has a friendly flow,
And wisdom found in a leaf on the ground,
Is often wrapped in fun, you know.

The Hushed Heart of Nature

In the hush where the crickets play,
A grasshopper leaps, quite far away,
With shoes on his feet, a plan so neat,
Says, 'Life's a dance; come join the fray!'

The trees lean in to share their tales,
With winds that lift like friendly gales,
A parrot's squawk, on a hollowed rock,
Turns secrets into junk-mail trails.

Beneath the roots, a party brews,
With cupcakes made of morning dews,
While hedgehogs roast, the cream-filled toast,
And invite the owls for their evening news.

Each twig holds joy, a quirk or two,
In nature's heart, with mischief due,
So if you peek, through laughter's streak,
You'll find the truth is quite askew.

Secrets of the Clinging Green

In the clutches of green, a surprise unfurls,
With acorns dressed as shiny pearls,
A cat with a grin, claims it's a win,
For nature hides the funniest swirls.

The winds chuckle through leaves of jade,
As ivy whispers, 'You've got it made!'
With twirling twigs, like dancing pigs,
In this wild, green escapade.

A whimsy blooms where shadows drape,
With secrets formed in a jester's cape,
A turtle in style, with a cheeky smile,
Says, 'Come for the laughs, and stay for the shape!'

So wander near the clinging vines,
And hear the chuckles as laughter shines,
For nature's art is wise and smart,
And joy is found in playful lines.

The Allure of Wild Growth

In a garden, green and bold,
Tales of mischief start to unfold.
Plants dance round with teasing grace,
Chasing bugs in a funny race.

Bees wear hats, all quite absurd,
While flowers gossip without a word.
Vines twist and giggle in the breeze,
Joking with the bending trees.

The carrots wear their leafy crowns,
While radishes parade through the towns.
Bumblebees buzz with playful cheer,
Tickling petals, spreading good cheer.

In this patch of wild delight,
Life is whimsical, pure, and bright.
Nature's laughter fills the air,
Causing giggles everywhere.

Bound by Nature's Embrace

Two plants argue, who grew the best?
The sunflower claims it's all a jest.
The ivy chuckles, stays in their shade,
While the daisies dance in the parade.

"Look at me! I twist and climb,"
Said the vine with confidence, feeling sublime.
"Just wait and see, I'll reach the sun,
While you all argue, I'll have my fun!"

The snails race slow, yet think they're fast,
While bunnies munch on greens amassed.
Each creature in this leafy space,
Finds joy in nature's warm embrace.

With leaves that flutter and roots that hug,
Each growth, it seems, gives a playful tug.
Life's a dance, an amusing chase,
In harmony, they find their place.

The Garden's Secret Keeper

In the corner, secrets thrive,
As trowels chat, the garden's alive.
The mulch whispers of plans gone awry,
While willows sway and begin to sigh.

"Did you hear what happened with the peas?"
Asked the pot, in a voice like a tease.
"They tried to grow up, but lost their way,
Got tangled in weeds, oh what a day!"

Cabbages wear their heads held high,
Feeling regal beneath the sky.
While everything plots in leafy delight,
Underground wonders take to flight.

Peeking through, a creature winks,
As tomatoes ponder, or so it thinks.
Laughter echoes from root to bloom,
In this garden, there's always room.

A Symphony of Climbing Dreams

Vines crescendo, reaching for grace,
Scale the fence, set a quick pace.
Trellises groan with leafy delight,
As blossoms compete, what a funny sight!

On the ground, chatterbugs sing,
While the grasshoppers leap in a spring.
"Catch me if you can!" they boldly declare,
As butterflies twirl in the warm air.

Each twig tells a story bizarre,
From the whispers of the moon to the stars.
Laughter ripples through branches wide,
Nature's concert, there's nothing to hide.

In harmony, they sway and glow,
A whimsical rhythm, a garden show.
With each climb comes a giddy cheer,
In the symphony of dreams, we all draw near.

Leaves Holding Time's Fragments

In a garden where socks fester,
Dandelions throw a raucous jester.
Each leaf whispers tales of old,
While gnomes trade secrets 'neath the bold.

Chasing shadows, laughter bounces,
The trees giggle as time flounces.
With every wiggle of the vine,
A timepiece lost in garden twine.

A creeping crawl awaits the hare,
Who stops to chat with lady fair.
They ponder where the lost shoes lay,
In leafy realms where squirrels play.

When autumn leaves begin to tease,
The critters laugh, they dance with ease.
For every tick of nature's clock,
A funny peek from clever stock.

Beneath the Canopy's Gaze

Underneath the leaf-rimmed skies,
Squirrels jest, with mischievous eyes.
They hide acorns near the roots,
Thinking they hold nature's truths.

Frogs croak out their ribbit songs,
While flies buzz 'round, they croon along.
The trees chuckle, swaying slow,
At mischief brewing down below.

A snail wearing sunglasses slides,
As caterpillars spin wild rides.
The laughter echoes, branches sway,
In leafy realms where critters play.

Beneath the canopy so wide,
Nature's jesters take their pride.
A world of laughs, a joyful dance,
In shades of green, they twirl and prance.

The Cryptic Embrace of Nature

Twisted vines in a waltz combine,
Whispering secrets, oh how they twine!
A creeping joke behind each bark,
Where shadows night take on a spark.

With every curl and playful twist,
The bushes conspire, none can resist.
A fox with shades, struts down the lane,
While rabbits plot pranks to entertain.

Mushrooms giggle at the troll,
Who trips on roots, lost in his stroll.
Peaceful whispers of ancient trees,
Share punchlines carried on the breeze.

In nature's crypt where secrets lie,
Each creature shares a witty sigh.
A comedic twist in every bloom,
As life unfolds—no room for gloom.

Thorns of Solitude

In a garden filled with prickly charms,
Lonely roses hide their sharp arms.
They sigh, "Who needs friends, it's fine,"
While bees buzz close, a funny line.

A cactus quips with a pointed grin,
"Welcome to my home, do come in!"
While wild things laugh, quite at ease,
In solitude, they share their tease.

The thorns, they giggle, who would've thought?
That lonely hearts can still be caught.
With each petal, a ticklish plea,
For someone to join in on the spree.

So here they grow, in light and shade,
The thorns tell tales of jokes well made.
For even in solitude, they find,
A laugh, a jest, nature's sweet kind.

Shadows in the Garden

In the garden at dawn, shadows play,
Leaves whisper secrets, come what may.
A gnome winks, guarding his prize,
While daisies giggle, under bright skies.

A squirrel debates with a butterfly,
Who's faster at dodging the passersby.
Marigolds dance with comical flair,
As the wind tousles each flower's hair.

A hedgehog rolls, trying to hide,
From the giggling daisies, who burst with pride.
The sun chuckles low, a warm embrace,
As shadows ballet in this silly place.

In this garden, life's a riot,
Where even the weeds try to keep it quiet.
Each petal and stem in a joyful spree,
Doing the tango, wild and free.

Conspiracy of Green

A plan unfolds where no one sees,
The cabbages plot over cups of peas.
Amongst the sprouts, low whispers churn,
While garlic bulbs plot, waiting their turn.

The lettuce nods, with a wink so sly,
"Shall we trellis the tomatoes? Oh my!"
Radishes roll laughing down the row,
It seems they have a trick up their sleeve, you know!

A rogue zucchini struts with flair,
As tiny herbs stifle giggles to share.
Petunias gossip, swirling around,
In this green conspiracy, joy is found.

So take a peek in this leafy plot,
You might find laughter that can't be bought.
In this garden of chatter and playful schemes,
Even the weeds are living their dreams.

Veil of Climbing Shadows

A vine creeps up, doing its best,
To hide behind trellises, all in jest.
It tickles the fence, has the best laugh,
Taking photos with the garden path.

Under the cover of leafy disguise,
Giggling blossoms share silly lies.
A cucumber on stilts claims it's so grand,
While peas in pods form a marching band.

Twisted around are secrets so bright,
As critters play hide and seek in the light.
The shadows play tricks, oh what a sight,
As the garden comes alive with delight.

In this realm where the green things tease,
Every climbing vine aims to please.
Join the laughter, let the humor grow,
In this garden where silliness flows.

Hidden Gems of the Trellis

Up high on the trellis, a secret unfolds,
With stories of veggies that never grow old.
Peppers and squash, all in a row,
Laugh as they dress in the best garden show.

A vine juggles fruits, oh what a sight,
While herbs crack jokes, full of delight.
Tomatoes grumble, "We're ripe, can't you see?"
As the carrots snicker, "Just wait, let us be!"

Even the radishes hide in their roles,
Planning a heist with playful goals.
As the sun dips low, the gossip explodes,
In this vibrant patch where laughter codes.

So stroll through this garden, full of surprise,
Where every plant beams with sparkly eyes.
From tiny seeds to the tallest vine,
Hidden gems twinkle, all are divine.

Sentinels of the Shaded Path

In the garden where greens entwine,
Ivy whispers tales divine.
Sneaky squirrels make their rounds,
Under leaves, no one sounds.

Bees are buzzing, oh what a laugh,
Old stones smile—time's photograph.
One cat napping, nestle so tight,
While critters dance in the moonlight.

Sunlight dapples, shadows play,
Nature's jesters in full sway.
A loose leaf tickles a toe,
"Who did that?" They all want to know!

Creeping vines tease all who pass,
Poking fun at iron grass.
With a chuckle, flowers bloom,
In this secluded, green-lit room.

The Lore of Climbing Nature

Listen close, there's fun to find,
Climbing plants, oh, they unwind!
A twisty story, laughs abound,
In leafy laughter, joy is found.

One little tendril gave a shout,
Swung from branches in and out.
"Catch me if you can!" it sang,
As nature's laughter loudly rang.

A squirrel slipped, but landed right,
On a twig—it gave a fright!
The ivy giggled, roots held tight,
In the chaos, all took flight.

Frogs in chorus, croaking trends,
Join the leaves—they're all good friends.
This climb of nature, full of glee,
Invites all to join, you see!

In the Heart of Verdancy

In verdant depths where shadows creep,
A network hides, but not too deep.
Mischief dances on every vine,
With giggles that remain divine.

Lizards basking, colorful and spry,
Play hide-and-seek as butterflies fly.
"Found you!" cries a leaf, with glee,
"Come play again, just wait and see!"

Wobbling grasshoppers join the scene,
Turning moments into a green screen.
Nature's chuckles fill the air,
A playful heart, no need to care.

Each step taken on this path,
Brings giggles, joy, and lots of laughs.
A leafy cradle sways in the breeze,
Whispering secrets, laughing with ease.

Secrets of the Sinuous Path

On twisting trails where laughter flows,
A hidden tale in ivy grows.
With every twist and every turn,
A foot will trip, but still we learn.

"Follow me," a vine will tease,
As butterflies dance with perfect ease.
In colorful bloom, they flap about,
Playful whispers, no room for doubt.

A frog leaps forth with quite a splash,
With giggles and hops, it makes a dash.
"Oh dear!" we chuckle, "not again!"
Nature's jesters delight in our pain!

As shadows lengthen, humor shows,
In every petal, laughter grows.
Through this path, we ride the jest,
In secret gardens, we're truly blessed.

The Path Less Grown

In the garden where no one goes,
A patch of weeds steals the show.
They dance and twirl with glee,
A leafy party, just let it be!

A rare tree thought to be a frown,
Wears a necklace of green, quite the crown.
It whispers jokes to the flower nearby,
"Don't worry, I'm just too shy to fly!"

The bugs all gather, make quite a scene,
Complain about the lack of beans.
They share their tales of woe and bliss,
Amidst the clover's green abyss.

So if you stumble on this humorous plot,
Join in the laughter, give it a shot.
For even plants can have a spree,
In this wild, weedy jubilee!

Beneath the Enshrouded Arbour

Underneath the leafy dome,
Squirrels are scheming, far from home.
They plot with crows, play tricks on bees,
Creating chaos with the greatest of ease.

The shadows chuckle, branches sway,
As acorns roll in a merry ballet.
A chipmunk slips on a greased-up nut,
Squeaking loudly, "Stuck in a rut!"

Beneath this canopy, secrets spun,
Where spindly vines have too much fun.
They play tag with the dappled light,
And giggle into the cool of night.

So if you peer in this leafy place,
Expect some giggles, maybe a race.
For nature's jesters abound and play,
In their own greenish, silly way!

The Silent Witness Above

Up high in branches, the owls all grin,
Watching the antics and chaos within.
"Who, who!" they ask with curious stare,
As the raccoons throw a wild hair affair.

A flash of feathers, a fluttering show,
As sparrows chirp and put on a flow.
"Look at me!" an overconfident thrush,
Sings loudly while crashing in a bush.

Their night-time revels echo loud,
As critters gather, a rambunctious crowd.
And above it all, from their elevated perch,
The wise old owls begin to lurch.

With laughter ringing through the trees,
They craft the night into a breeze.
For even creatures up high and proud,
Can't help but chuckle at the raucous crowd!

Veils of Verdant Mystery

In tangled vines where no one treads,
A turtle pondered, bumping its head.
"Why try to hide?" it sighed with glee,
"When I could just be, wild and free!"

The foliage rustles, whispers abound,
As ladybugs dance all around.
They giggle and tease, in a colorful parade,
A wild garden, their merry charade.

A hidden treasure? A garden gnome!
Turned upside down, searching for home.
"Where's my hat?" he moans in despair,
The daisies laugh, "It's under there!"

So embrace the mystery that creeps and crawls,
In the play of shadows, hilarity calls.
For beneath the leaves, with each silly scene,
Lies the joy of nature's whimsical green!

Intertwined Tales of the Wild

In the garden, plants do gossip,
With bright green laughter, so they frolic.
A rose rolled her eyes at a thorny tale,
While daisies danced with a melodious wail.

The mushrooms grinned in their huddled space,
As the jasmine swayed with a charming grace.
A dandelion puffed up, full of pride,
Saying, "My seeds can travel worldwide!"

A geranium blushed at a bee's sweet hey,
Chasing butterflies who liked to play.
Together they spun the sun's lazy beams,
In a wild world filled with such absurd dreams.

With laughter and color, they took a stand,
A curious crew in this plant-based band.
No secrets kept, just tales and glee,
In the vine-covered realms where nature runs free.

The Forgotten Archive of Flora

Once upon a time in a leafy nook,
Lived a sage old fern with a dusty book.
Each page was filled with stories so rare,
Of flowers that danced and trees that could stare.

The lilies giggled, their petals abloom,
As they recited the tales of their gloom.
With a pluck and a wink, the violets chimed,
"We're not forgettable, just well-timed!"

A cactus yelled, "Wait, do I get a line?"
Yet his prickly demeanor was quite a sign.
The basil, so spicy, threw in a pun,
While the thistle just pricked everyone for fun!

In this archive of giggles, love, and tricks,
Flora's secrets became clever flicks.
So if you hear whispers in your next stroll,
It's just the plants having fun on a roll!

Whispers Among the Vines

In the trellis where the grapevines twine,
They whisper tales over a glass of wine.
With a wink and a nod, they tease the wind,
While pesky squirrels plot where they'll send.

A sweet pea sighed, "Oh, the stories I know!"
About a cat who thought he could grow.
The berries laughed, bursting with cheer,
And a cheeky tomato chimed, "I am here!"

Vines wrapped together, a tangled show,
Creating a scene, full of mirth and glow.
The leaves all chuckled at a seed's big plan,
To sprout a dance that no one can can!

So next time you wander past the green,
Listen closely to what you've not seen.
For amidst the laughter, what can you find?
Just whispers of fun that nature designed!

Enigma Beneath the Leaves

Beneath the canopy where shadows play,
A riddle formed in the light of day.
The ferns discussed who had the best style,
While the bark beetles plotted a wild trial.

A funny old oak shared tales of the past,
With acorns giggling, their time went fast.
"I've been here since Newton dropped that fruit!"
The willow wiggled in a leafy suit.

Each rustle above brought a delightful tease,
As crickets chirped, saying, "Life's a breeze!"
A root took a nap while the sun was high,
Dreaming of mischief that danced in the sky.

So if you should wander in this green maze,
Pause for a moment, let nature amaze.
For beneath the leaves, the laughter is grand,
In enigmas of fun that nature has planned.

Green Veils and Whispers

In the garden where shadows play,
Leaves conspire in a leafy ballet.
Laughter echoes through twisted vines,
While sneaky roots craft secret signs.

A beetle wears a tiny hat,
Debating with a lazy cat.
They toast with dew drops all around,
As plants giggle at the sound.

Frogs in bow ties leap with glee,
Inviting ants to share some tea.
A sunflower cracks a sunflower joke,
And all around, the garden stokes.

Here, whispers dance and mischief thrives,
In a world where humor arrives.
With every grumble, bloom, and sprout,
The secret laughs, and we all shout!

The Hidden Dialogue of Growth

In the soil, a chat takes root,
Between a sprout and a leafy brute.
"Hey, do you hear that buzzing sound?"
"Just the honeycombs going around!"

A daisy rolls its eyes in fun,
As snails race under the sun.
"I'm faster, wait—no, you're too slow!"
"By next spring, I'll steal the show!"

The mushrooms gather for a feast,
With jokes that sprout like wild yeast.
"Can fungi dance?" they joke and snicker,
While giggling roots pull on the ticker.

In this dialogue of leaves and lore,
Nature's laughter fills the floor.
While garden critics root for more,
The comedy blooms forevermore!

Fragments of Forgotten Flora

Once stood a plant with tales to share,
But lost its voice somewhere in the air.
A dandelion, bold and spry,
Cracks up, "I just can't tell a lie!"

The roses wink with petals bright,
Trading puns in soft moonlight.
"What did the weed say to the sprout?"
"Quit clowning around, let's figure it out!"

Amid the patches and buzzing flies,
Cacti giggle, casting sly sighs.
"Stick around—let's share a joke!
I've got a prickly one, let it poke!"

Fragments dance, stories unfold,
In harmony, laughter's bold.
These plants know how to have their fun,
Come share their cosmos—everyone!

Guardians of the Overgrown

In the wild where the brambles grow,
There's a council of plants, don't you know?
They guard their turf with wit and cheer,
Plotting pranks for all to hear.

"Have you seen the squirrel in a tie?"
"Did he finally learn how to fly?"
Breezes halt to catch their banter,
As flowers bloom, a colorful canter.

With ivy hats and stems of glee,
They host a dance—come one, come three!
"Do the waggle and twist, not so fast!
We're guardians—make this laugh last!"

In every thicket, whispers remain,
Of fun and jest amid the pain.
In every leaf, a chuckle found,
These guardians keep joy renowned!

Secrets Entwined in Silence

In a garden where whispers creep,
Lurking vines plot and scheme, you see.
A leaf wants to dance but can't find the beat,
While the roots chuckle, a giggling spree.

Laughter bubbles beneath the moss,
As twigs join in, tossing sass and gloss.
They gossip at night, oh what a loss,
For sneaky is nature, a whimsical toss.

A Tapestry of Tendrils

Tendrils twist with playful glee,
Stitching tales on the old oak tree.
Every curl holds a joke, oh me!
Who knew green could have such esprit?

The branches nod at the stories spun,
A party where the leaves do run.
Nature's festival, no need for a gun,
Just a leaf blower to ruin the fun!

The Veil of Verdant Grace

Under a curtain of leafy laughter,
A squirrel plays the role of master.
With acorns piled like a jester's hat,
His antics leave the garden in a splatter.

Peeking through ferns, a shy branch sighs,
As buzzing bees hum secret alibis.
All while the daisies roll their eyes,
In this lush world, mischief never dies.

Beneath the Climbing Shadows

Shadows wiggle with shimmy and sway,
As vines explore by the light of day.
A flower sneezes, pollen flies away,
While grumpy toadstools just grumble and say.

The moon overhears their leafy jokes,
While busy ants scurry like a bunch of dopes.
All woven in laughter, a tapestry of yokes,
In the garden of giggles, the humor evokes.

The Tangle of Old Lore

In the garden, tales entwine,
Old vines whisper, slightly divine.
Where gnomes dance in silly twirls,
And secrets bloom like painted pearls.

A squirrel claims the throne of leaves,
Debating with the buzzing bees.
They argue who's the queen or king,
While spiders laugh and spin their string.

A lazy cat snores on the ground,
As hidden pranks are all around.
The flowers giggle, their petals flap,
While frogs do waltzes, fancy and tap.

So come and join this leafy spree,
Where laughter drips from every tree.
In crazy corners, secrets curl,
A tangle of fun in this old world.

Threads of Hidden Stories

Oh, the stories that we weave,
In the treetops, hard to believe.
With every loop a giggle spills,
As nature sings and pokes with quills.

A gossiping owl spins a tale,
Of the raccoon's nocturnal sail.
With acorns stacked in many piles,
And fairies prancing in bright styles.

The winds do curl and whisper loud,
While daffodils giggle with the crowd.
They sway and conspire with roots unseen,
Where sunlight dances, bold and keen.

Each thread of green holds a jest,
As bunnies hop in a woolly vest.
These hidden tales in twisty threads,
Bring forth the laughter as long as it spreads.

Verdant Whispers of Time

In the green embrace of ancient vines,
Where whispers build their foolish shrines.
A turtle tells his slow-paced tale,
While butterflies resend the mail.

The ivy's pranks and giggles bloom,
Trapped in the garden's vibrant room.
Mice plan a dance on the old stone wall,
As shadows turn to a merry ball.

With beetles dressed in tiny threads,
And ladybugs aboard their beds.
They hold an auction for the best,
Of sunflower seeds, a veggie fest!

So listen close, the earth's a hoot,
Each twist and turn a funny root.
In verdant whispers, time does play,
Among the leaves where odd things stay.

Guardians of the Hidden Grove

In a grove where mischief brews,
Stand guardians who share their views.
A raccoon dressed in dapper style,
Cracks jokes that can take a while.

A hedgehog rolls with laughter's glee,
As chipmunks host a comedy spree.
While shadows slip and antics flare,
The trees all chuckle in the air.

The toads play cards on a mossy throne,
With wild rules that are all their own.
They bet on flies and yodel loud,
Creating quite the quirky crowd.

This hidden grove, a laughing place,
Where nature shows its furry face.
As secrets slip and giggles soar,
The guardians dance just like before.

Tendrils of a Forgotten Past

In the garden where shadows play,
A plant insists it knows the way.
It twists and turns, a comical sight,
Claiming wisdom, oh what a plight!

Once a vine with tales to tell,
Now it sprawls and does quite well.
Yet, as it grows, it starts to prance,
Caught in a dance, oh what a chance!

The neighbors laugh, they think it wise,
But the plant just dreams of oversized pies.
A chef in training, it steals the show,
A leafy chef in a potpourri glow!

Oh tiny tendrils and leaves so green,
What secrets hide in your leafy sheen?
Fill our hearts with laughter, dear friend,
And twist and twine till the very end!

The Language of Twining Stems

In a world where stems start to tease,
They wiggle and giggle in the breeze.
Sprouting jokes from the soil below,
Helping the flowers to steal the show!

Whispers of twine tickle the air,
Leaves throw tantrums; all must beware!
A silliness blooms with every curl,
Twirling and swirling, oh what a whirl!

With each tendril, a punchline grows,
Unraveling tales as laughter flows.
"Oh, what's that?" they ask with a grin,
"A green comedian! Let the fun begin!"

Laughter rooted in nature's schemes,
Twisting humor beneath sunny beams.
In the dance of caps and leaves so bold,
The language of laughter still unfolds.

Shades of Mystery in the Arbor

In the depths of the shady grove,
Vines plot mischief, oh how they rove!
Shrouded in secrets, they exchange a glance,
A leafy gossip in a viney dance!

"Did you hear the joke that Oak just told?"
Said the sly creeper, bold and cold.
"They say the roots danced last night in fright,
Just to scare off a raccoon's delight!"

Giggling softly, the branches sway,
While hidden critters join the play.
A chorus of chuckles from the leafy boughs,
As nature skips and takes a bow!

With every twist, a mystery deep,
In the trees where the whispers creep.
Secrets shared with a chuckle and grin,
In shades of green, let the fun begin!

A Chorus of Leafy Whispers

In a chorus of leaves, voices rise,
Each tiny whisper, a grand surprise.
"Who's the funniest plant, do you think?"
"Oh, that prickly cactus, we all need a drink!"

Greenery giggles, gossiping under the sun,
As vines recite jokes — oh what fun!
"Why did the leaf refuse to play?
It couldn't find a branch for the fray!"

With tendrils entwined, laughter unfurls,
As the petals shimmy and twirl and swirl.
"Let's start a band, with roots on the bass!
We'll rock the garden and win the race!"

So raise a glass to the leafy lot,
For in their whispers, joy is caught.
In the verdant theater, each pun takes flight,
A symphony of laughter, pure delight!

The Language of Leaves

Whispers tangled in the trees,
A gossip shared by rustling leaves.
They gossip of squirrels, coy and sly,
And the cat who thinks he can fly.

In the courtyard, secrets unfold,
As petals spin tales, bold yet cold.
The dandelions chuckle with glee,
While the daisies roll their eyes at a bee.

Branches twist in a playful dance,
Each leaf a part of a leafy romance.
Beneath the shade, where shadows play,
There's mischief brewed at the close of day.

So listen closely to the green above,
Nature's humor in a leaf-clad grove.
For trees will sing, in their own cheeky way,
Of laughter that holds the world at bay.

Beneath the Thicket

Beneath the thicket, gnomes convene,
Telling jokes that are rarely seen.
A snail laughs, his humor slow,
While mice snicker at a crow's faux pas show.

The mushrooms wear hats of polka dot,
Swapping tales that twist and knot.
A chipmunk jests with a bashful grin,
About his race to the top of a tin.

Bumblebees buzz with witty charm,
As clovers cast spells, a dose of calm.
Underneath the thicket, absurdity blooms,
With chortles and chuckles, it lightens the glooms.

So wander down and lend an ear,
To all the whispers of fun you'll hear.
For nature's jest is a potent brew,
That blooms in green, just for you.

Enchanted Overgrowth

In the heart of the wild, where chaos sings,
The overgrowth plays with mysterious things.
A hedgehog donned in a bow tie neat,
Holds court with flowers; it's quite the feat.

Vines twist, and the daisies prance,
Each telling tales of a peculiar dance.
Birds chirp laughter, as they flutter by,
While crickets compose a chorus that's spry.

A patch of mint has something to say,
About roguish ants that come out to play.
A wild rhubarb has clever flares,
Daring the others to compare their wares.

So venture forth into this mirth,
Where humor grows right from the earth.
In enchanted overgrowth, let's unite,
For nature's jest is a sheer delight.

Unraveling the Green

In the midst of the meadow, green threads unwind,
Weaving tales that are one of a kind.
With each unravel, a chuckle escapes,
As snickering moss pulls playful drapes.

Fern fronds flutter, like dancers, they sway,
While toadstools chat about yesterday.
A cheeky beetle claims he's a star,
While ants throw a party, raising the bar.

The willow whispers secrets from trees,
Of fish that got away with the breeze.
Each stalk and blade has a punchline in tow,
Waiting for listeners to join in the show.

So tread with glee through this maze of green,
Where nature's humor can always be seen.
Unravel the joy, let it burst like the sun,
For in every leaf lies laughter and fun.

Nature's Silent Confidant

In a garden where whispers dwell,
Plants gossip like they're under a spell.
Leaves tickle the breeze with laughter,
While bees buzz with joyful chatter.

A squirrel overhears, nods with delight,
Jumping at jokes, a comical sight.
Rabbits roll by, ears perked up high,
As flowers burst forth, spreading their sighs.

The sun peeks through, a curious spy,
Listening in as the petals reply.
Nature's laughter rings, oh what a scene,
In this leafy world, there's mischief unseen.

Gossip of roots, tales of the dew,
Every twist and turn holds laughter anew.
In this vibrant realm, everything's clear,
Nature's a stand-up, if you lend her an ear.

Echoes Amongst the Climbing Foliage

An ivy climbed up a brick wall,
But her jokes seemed to fall, fall, fall.
"Why did the window close?" she told,
"Because it wanted a change from the old!"

A vine chimed in with a voice so sweet,
"Why do trees hate tests? They can't handle the heat!"
Together they laughed, a leafy spree,
Echoes of giggles among the tree.

The shadows danced with borrowed grace,
As twining green shared a warm embrace.
"Do you hear the whispers of the mist?"
"I do, they're secrets we shouldn't resist!"

Through the rustling leaves, the jokes would sail,
Chasing away clouds like a playful gale.
In the green, oh what funny tales soar,
Nature's own stand-up, forever encore!

The Tale of Climbing Empires

A small plant once dreamed of great heights,
"Why not conquer the wall?" she invites.
With each little tendril, she plotted her scheme,
"Soon I'll be queen, it'll be quite the scene!"

Her brother laughed, said, "Don't be absurd,
Climbing up there? You've not even stirred!"
But with a wink and a twist of her vine,
She whispered, "Just watch me, I'll truly shine!"

The neighboring flowers cheered her on,
As she twirled and twinkled from dusk until dawn.
A kingdom of leaves, a castle of green,
Empire of laughter, the best ever seen!

With every inch gained, there were selfies and cheers,
"Climbing queen, tell us your fears!"
"Only that someday, I'll need more sunscreen,
For I'll be the tallest that you've ever seen!"

Cobwebs of Greenery

In the corners of compassion, cobwebs sway,
"Are they friends or just lost?" the leaves often say.
A spider spun tales, sparkly and bright,
"Shall we throw in some bugs for a magical night?"

"Why are cobwebs so sticky?" a young bud inquired,
"To trap all the gossip," the old tree admired.
"Don't you see? This laughter's our glue,
Without a good joke, the fun would be few!"

Vines twisted in giggles, sharing their lore,
Of crickets who danced and ants who wore lore.
"Life's all about balance, let's have a blast,
Between all the cobwebs, let joy hold fast!"

So they hosted a party, in leaves and in light,
Where every bold leaf had a quip and a sight.
With laughter, the cobwebs hung soft as a dream,
In a world full of green, where humor is supreme.

www.ingramcontent.com/pod-product-compliance
Lightning Source LLC
Chambersburg PA
CBHW070320120526
44590CB00017B/2750